Cooking with Herbs and Spices

JOSCELINE DIMBLEBY

A SAINSBURY COOKBOOK

Published by Woodhead-Faulkner Limited
8 Market Passage, Cambridge CB2 3PF
for J Sainsbury Limited
Stamford House, Stamford Street, London SE1 9LL

First published 1979
© Josceline Dimbleby 1979
ISBN 0 85941 125 7

Cover design and text layout: Ken Vail
Colour photography and cover picture: Barry Bullough

Typesetting: Bedford Typesetters Limited
Printed and bound in Great Britain by
Hazell Watson and Viney Limited, Aylesbury, Bucks

Contents

Introduction

'New dishes beget new appetites.'
John Ray, 1627–1705

We are living through an exciting moment in the history of food in England. After many bland, unadventurous years herbs and spices are creeping back into English kitchens.

Up until the beginning of the nineteenth century a large variety of flavourings were available and used extensively in English households. But gradually the cooks cut down their use of herbs and spices so that until recently it was hard to find anything other than dried parsley, sage, thyme and mint, while spices would be restricted to nutmeg, cinnamon and cloves, which were used only at Christmas time. But now, partly because of the increased popularity of foreign foods but also because of the renewed enthusiasm and interest of the English in cookery, it is once again possible to find all sorts of unusual ingredients and flavourings to enhance our dishes. The gastronomic revival has really begun.

In India, the Far and the Middle East, South America and many European countries the addition of herbs and spices is part of everyday cooking, but each country uses them in their own way to achieve quite different effects. We in England, learning to use these new flavourings, are lucky to be able to borrow ideas from all these places while trying out experiments of our own, too.

The exciting and varying effect of herbs and spices on food was what first fired my enthusiasm for cookery. It is still my favourite kind of cooking. It seems to me magical that a little pinch of this or that can transform a dish from one thing to another, from the mundane to the exotic or from the indifferent to the excellent. It is intriguing to learn to identify the flavours and smells which, once you get accustomed to using them, can bring endless additions and variations to your cooking repertoire. As the taste of food lies largely in its smell, the aroma of different herbs and spices can work miracles with foods which before have always seemed rather dull.

When you can get them, the flavour of fresh herbs is undoubtedly best, but some freeze-dried herbs such as oregano, thyme and chives are most successful. Even if you have no garden you can gain great satisfaction from growing a selection of fresh herbs in a window box. Then, if you own a freezer you can enjoy the taste of fresh herbs all winter long. One useful way to freeze herbs is to chop them and pack a good teaspoonful at a time into ice cube trays, topping up with water to hold the herbs together once frozen. Keep the frozen cubes in plastic bags and label them carefully. Then, when a recipe suggests a teaspoonful of a certain herb, you just add a frozen cube. But for sprinkling herbs on to dishes and for garnishing it is better to freeze them without water, putting them into small plastic bags or pots. Unfortunately, frozen herbs will never be as sprightly as fresh herbs and will turn limp on thawing, but the flavour, which is the most important thing, will still be there.

In the recipes throughout the book I have given precise measurements for the addition of garlic, herbs or spices. Please remember that this can only be a guide: the exact flavour of the final result should be your own decision. The strength of herbs and spices varies with age and condition and you must always taste as you add and taste again at the end of the cooking, adjusting if you think it necessary. It is no good just throwing herbs and spices indiscriminately into dishes in the belief that they will be improved. Different flavours have a definite affinity with certain ingredients and this book is designed to give varied examples of this in both savoury and sweet dishes.

You will see that I recommend just a salad instead of a

cooked vegetable with many of the main dishes. This is a matter of taste but my feeling is that with spicy and well-flavoured or rich food a salad is more complementary and refreshing. And, of course, if you are entertaining it is much more relaxing if you don't have to be cooking vegetables at the last moment.

I have added a short guide, below, to the character of the various herbs and spices used in the recipes, and suggestions for their use, but the aim of the book is to encourage you to approach all food with curiosity and inventiveness. The most rewarding aspect of cooking with herbs and spices is that through experiment one is always discovering happy marriages between certain flavours, so that even familiar food takes on a new life.

Herbs

Bay leaves Can be used either fresh or dried. They go well with almost anything, including sweet dishes. Especially good boiled with milk to flavour cream puddings and custards.

Basil My favourite herb. A beautifully subtle and aromatic flavour. Use it fresh when available, or dried, to transform any tomato dish, pasta, eggs and fish, meat, sauces and salads. In fact, an addict will use basil with almost anything!

Chives A mild 'oniony' flavour. Good with eggs and cheese, sauces, soups and any delicately flavoured dishes. Makes a very pretty garnish.

Dill An important herb to look for. Both the leaves and seeds can be used but they have quite different flavours. Dill leaves are best known for their use in pickling cucumbers but they are lovely in salads and sprinkled on to cooked meat dishes and hot or cold fish dishes. Especially delicious added to delicate sauces and with cream and prawns. The seeds have a much stronger flavour, slightly like that of carraway seeds, but are good with boiled potatoes and cooked with pork.

Garlic At its best fairly fresh, with hard, plump cloves. In my opinion the most useful flavouring of all, as it goes with almost anything. It is also exceedingly healthy, as it is said to tone up the digestive system, reduce blood pressure and clear bronchitis.

Mint Easier than anything to grow fresh. Can be used in both savoury and sweet dishes. Classically used in England in mint sauce with lamb but also effective added to stews, chopped finely in meatballs, with chicken and sprinkled over vegetables.

Oregano and Marjoram Oregano is sometimes known as wild marjoram and the wild marjoram which grows in England is very similar to it. It has a rather stronger flavour than the cultivated English marjoram. Good with a great variety of dishes. Goes especially well with eggs, cheese, tomatoes, mushrooms, fish, and with minced pork and beef. Marjoram has a sweeter flavour and can be used in the same way as oregano, but is also good with liver and added sparingly to milk puddings.

Parsley Always useful, a health-giving herb which has never been out of favour. An indispensable garnish (especially the straight, fern-leaf, type) for flavouring numerous dishes. Particularly good with hot and cold sauces.

Rosemary A useful herb, since it is available fresh all year long. Good for roast lamb, pork and chicken and in all kinds of casseroles. Pretty used as a garnish. Gives a delicate flavour to sweet milk puddings and sauces if you boil a sprig with the milk.

Tarragon One of the great culinary herbs. Particularly good with chicken, vegetables, fish and cheese, in salads and for flavouring wine vinegar. Chop finely and add sparingly to subtle creamy sauces and cream soups.

Thyme Another of the great culinary herbs, used by the ancient Greeks and probably earlier. It is a pungent herb and particularly good for slow-cooking meat and game stews, and for stuffings and sauces. Sprigs of thyme impart a wonderful aroma when pushed into incisions in a joint of lamb before roasting.

Sage Often only associated with sage and onion stuffing, but it can be used in many ways. Good with veal and pork, in cheese and egg dishes, and in beef stews – in fact, at its best with any rich, aromatic dish.

Spices

Cardamom seeds My favourite spice. Wonderful in both savoury and sweet dishes and a vital spice in curry. It is an expensive spice, but pungent and aromatic, so that you need only a little at a time. Remove the seeds from the pods and grind them finely. Try them with casseroles, roast meats and minced meat, and in sauces. Irresistible in creamy puddings and ice creams.

Cayenne pepper Ground from the red chilli pepper and very hot. Use pinches in egg dishes and cheese sauces.

Chilli powder This is usually a mixture of ground chillies and other spices and varies in its hotness, so add sparingly and taste for flavour and strength. Best known as an important ingredient in curries and for the Mexican *chilli con carne*, but try adding a pinch to egg dishes and tomato soup.

Cinnamon Sold either in curled strips of bark or ready-ground, it can be used in both sweet and savoury dishes. Well-known for enhancing apple pies and cakes but unfamiliar in this country as an exciting addition to chicken and lamb casseroles, roast lamb and duck.

Coriander The seeds are a mild aromatic spice which has been used in cooking for thousands of years. Best known here as a pickling spice. Roughly grind them and use with roast meats and chicken, in stews and with baked fish. If you plant the seeds you can grow the invaluable coriander leaves, which have quite a different flavour. They give an exotic taste to salads and are lovely chopped roughly and thrown into curries and stews at the last minute, and added to sauces.

Cumin seeds A distinctive and powerful spice not often used in European cooking but very effective with lamb stews or roasts and in meatballs. An important ingredient in curries.

Ginger This can be the familiar ground ginger, crystallised ginger or the aromatic fresh root ginger now available in England. Crystallised ginger is mostly used in sweet dishes and cakes but for savoury dishes use the fresh root ginger, if available, or the dried, ground variety. The root has to be peeled and chopped finely and has a fresh lemony smell, not at all what you normally associate with ginger. It is very aromatic and only pleasantly hot. Delicious with all kinds of meat and fish.

Green Chilli Fresh chillies are much more easy to find nowadays. They have both flavour and bite but be careful to extract all the little seeds, which are burning hot, and don't lick your fingers after touching them! Experiment by adding the finely chopped chilli sparingly to all kinds of dishes or smear a grilled steak with a broken piece of chilli instead of black pepper.

Nutmeg The flavour blends well with both sweet and savoury dishes and never dominates. Especially good added to creamed potatoes and swedes and to mild, creamy stews and sauces. Also good with spinach and cream cheeses. Whenever possible, use whole nutmeg, freshly ground.

Paprika This is a special red pepper ground finely, but free from the hotness of chilli or cayenne. It has a mild, sweetish flavour and can be used in generous quantities. It gives a lovely red colour. Use in sauces, stews and chicken, fish, egg and cheese dishes.

Turmeric A native of the ginger family, ground to a bright yellow powder and widely used in pickles, chutney and curry powders. It is good for rice dishes and used sparingly to colour and flavour all white sauces, soups and egg dishes.

Note on quantities

Ingredients in the recipes are given in both Imperial (oz, pints, etc) and metric (g, ml, etc) measures: use either set of quantities, but not a mixture of both, in any one recipe. All teaspoons and tablespoons are level spoons unless otherwise stated.

First Courses and Light Meals

'Variety's the very spice of life, that gives it all its flavour.'
William Cowper, 1731–1800

Leeks Cooked in Spiced Wine

Serves 4

A cold dish which makes a very simple but popular start to a meal. It also makes a good side dish to go with cold meat. Always serve with fresh brown bread to mop up the delicious juices.

4 large leeks
2 bay leaves
¼ pint (150 ml) white wine
1 teaspoon (5 ml spoon) pickling spice
2 tablespoons (2 × 15 ml spoon) olive oil
salt, black pepper

Take the outside leaves from the leeks and wash well. Cut each leek into 2–3-inch (5–7.5 cm) pieces and put into a wide saucepan with the rest of the ingredients and salt and black pepper to taste. Cover the dish and simmer very gently for 15–25 minutes or until the leeks are soft.

Arrange the leeks on a serving dish and strain the juices and spices over the top. Cool and then chill in the fridge before serving.

Smoked Haddock Soup

Serves 4

This is a deliciously creamy and delicate fish soup. If you add turmeric as suggested it will give the soup a lovely yellow colour and a more unusual flavour, but it is not essential. It is a perfect first course to a meal and good for a simple supper, too, accompanied by fresh wholemeal bread, warmed in the oven.

8 oz (225 g) smoked haddock, cod or whiting fillets
2 oz (50 g) butter or margarine
4 tablespoons (4 × 15 ml spoon) plain flour
1 teaspoon (5 ml spoon) turmeric (optional)
2 good pinches cayenne pepper
1 pint (600 ml) milk
1 pint (600 ml) water
6 fl oz (180 ml) single cream
juice of 1 small lemon
a good sprinkling of chopped fresh or dried chives
salt, black pepper

Let the fish thaw slightly if frozen and then skin it and cut it into very small cubes. Melt the butter in a fairly large, heavy-based saucepan. Stir in the fish, followed by the flour, the turmeric, if used, and the cayenne. Add, not too quickly, the milk and water.

Bring to the boil, stirring all the time, and then cover and simmer very gently, stirring once or twice, for 10–15 minutes. Remove from the heat, add the cream and very gradually stir in the lemon juice. Finally, add the chives and season to taste with salt and a little black pepper if desired.

Pea and Mint Soup

Serves 4–6

This smooth and refreshing soup, so simple to make, is equally good chilled or served hot. If you decide to have it hot, it is best accompanied by a bowl of grated Emmenthal, Jarlsberg or Fynbo cheese which people can sprinkle into their soup at the table.

3 oz (75 g) butter or margarine
1 small onion, chopped roughly
1–2 cloves garlic, chopped
a large handful of fresh mint leaves, chopped roughly
1 lb (450 g) shelled fresh or frozen peas
2 pints (1.1 litres) chicken stock
¼ pint (150 ml) single cream
juice of ½ small lemon
salt, black pepper

Melt the butter in a large saucepan. Add the onion, garlic, mint (saving a little for garnishing), peas and stock. Bring to the boil, cover and simmer gently for 10–15 minutes, or until the peas and the onions are tender. Allow to cool and blend in a liquidiser until very smooth. Add the cream and stir in the lemon juice very gradually. Season to taste with salt and black pepper.

Either chill in the fridge when cold, or reheat and serve hot. Sprinkle a little chopped mint on top before serving.

Carrot and Orange Soup

Serves 4

Served chilled and sprinkled with fresh chives this is a most refreshing soup, yet served hot with croûtons of fried bread it is rich and sustaining.

1½ lb (700 g) carrots
2–3 large whole cloves garlic, peeled
juice of 1 lemon
grated rind of 1, and juice of 3, oranges
1 pint (600 ml) water
¼ whole nutmeg, grated, or ¼ teaspoon (½ × 2.5 ml spoon) ground nutmeg
½ pint (300 ml) single cream
fresh chives, chopped, for garnish (optional)
salt, black pepper

Wash and scrape the carrots and cut up roughly. Put in a saucepan with the garlic, lemon juice, orange rind and water. Cover, bring to the boil and simmer for about half an hour, or until the carrots are soft. Add the nutmeg and leave to cool a little.

Add the orange juice and blend all in a liquidiser until smooth. Stir in the cream and season to taste with salt and black pepper.

Serve either reheated or chilled and sprinkled with chives (or a little grated carrot). If, when chilled, it seems too thick, stir in some milk.

A Selection of Soups: Smoked Haddock (see p. 14); Carrot and Orange; Pea and Mint (see p. 15)

Creamed Chicory and Avocado Salad

Serves 4–5

A delicious combination of texture and taste dressed with cream. This salad also makes a good first course accompanied by fresh wholemeal bread.

For the salad
2–3 heads of chicory
$\frac{1}{2}$ small cucumber
1 avocado
2 oz (50 g) hazelnut kernels

For the dressing
6 fl oz (180 ml) single cream
2 teaspoons (2 × 5 ml spoon) chopped fresh, or 1 teaspoon (5 ml spoon) dried, chives
salt, black pepper

Cut the chicory across in rounds. Peel the cucumber and cut into chunks. Cut the avocado in half, twist to separate, remove the stone, peel with a sharp knife and cut into chunks. Put all together in a salad bowl and scatter with the hazelnuts.

In a small bowl mix the cream with the chives and salt and black pepper to taste and dress the salad with this mixture.

Fish Rolls with Spanish Sauce

Serves 6

This unusual recipe makes a tempting first course or lunch party dish. Garlic, prawns and onions are wrapped in tender plaice and coated with a fresh tomato sauce.

For the rolls
4 oz (100 g) peeled prawns, roughly chopped
2 oz (50 g) flaked almonds
1 large clove garlic, crushed
6 small fillets of plaice
cooking oil
salt, black pepper

For the sauce
1 lb (450 g) tomatoes, dipped in boiling water and skinned
approx. 3 tablespoons (3 × 15 ml spoon) olive or sunflower
    oil
juice of 1 orange
1 tablespoon (15 ml spoon) dried oregano
1 large clove garlic, crushed
chopped fresh parsley or chives (or, best of all, fresh basil)
    to garnish
salt, black pepper

Heat the oven to Gas Mark 6/400°F/200°C.

Mix the prawns, almonds and the crushed garlic with salt and pepper in a bowl. Lay out the fillets of plaice and spoon some of the mixture on to each one. Roll the fillets over the stuffing, secure with a wooden toothpick (don't worry if a little stuffing tumbles out at either end) and arrange in a shallow, oiled, fireproof dish.

Brush the stuffed fillets with oil. Cover the dish with foil and bake in the centre of the oven for 20 minutes. Take out, drain off and reserve any juices, and leave to cool.

Meanwhile, cut the peeled tomatoes into small pieces and put them in a frying pan with the reserved fish juices, olive oil, orange juice, oregano, crushed garlic and salt and black pepper to taste. Cook very gently, stirring often until the tomatoes have gone mushy and the mixture has become a thick sauce. Cool in the pan and then stir again.

Carefully transfer the fish rolls to a serving dish, remove the toothpicks and scrape off the skin. Spoon the sauce over the fish and sprinkle with the parsley, chives or basil. Chill in the fridge before serving.

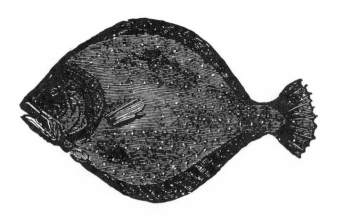

Fish Rolls with Spanish Sauce

Little Chive Pies

To make 18 pies

As a first course or for a party these little pies with light, rich pastry cannot fail to be popular. You can make them well in advance and keep them in the fridge, but you should serve them either slightly warm or at room temperature.

For the pastry
12 oz (350 g) strong plain flour
pinch of salt
6 oz (175 g) butter or margarine
3 oz (75 g) lard
milk to glaze pies

For the filling
8 oz (225 g) full fat cream cheese or curd cheese
2–3 teaspoons (2–3 × 5 ml spoon) chopped fresh, or 2
   teaspoons (2 × 5 ml spoon) dried, chives
salt, black pepper

Sift the flour and salt into a mixing bowl. Cut in the fat and rub in the mixture with your fingertips until it resembles breadcrumbs. With a knife, mix in a little cold water (about 4–5 tablespoons, 4–5 × 15 ml spoon) until the mixture just sticks together. Gather into a ball, wrap in foil and chill in the fridge for at least an hour.

Put the filling ingredients into a bowl and mix thoroughly together. To make the pies, roll out the pastry to about $\frac{1}{8}$ inch (4 mm) thickness. Use a 3-inch (7.5 cm) round fluted cutter and cut out 18 rounds, and then with a $2\frac{1}{4}$-inch (5.5 cm) round cutter cut another 18 rounds, re-rolling the pastry as necessary.

Line some patty tins with the large rounds. Smooth some filling into each round. Moisten the underside of the smaller rounds and put on top, pressing down lightly at the edges.

Heat the oven to Gas Mark 7/425°F/220°C. Cut a small

slit in the top of each pie. Brush with milk and bake in the centre of the oven for about 20 minutes. Leave to cool in the tins for 5–10 minutes and then gently – as the pastry is deliciously crumbly – ease them out with a round-bladed knife.

Spiced Eggs with Cucumber

Serves 4

Easy to make, this is a decorative first course. Stuffed eggs can taste very rich but in this case the crunchy pieces of cucumber are most refreshing.

4 hard-boiled eggs
2 oz (50 g) cream or curd cheese
2 teaspoons (2 × 5 ml spoon) lemon juice
1 oz (25 g) butter
¼ teaspoon (½ × 2.5 ml spoon) turmeric
¼ teaspoon (½ × 2.5 ml spoon) chilli powder
1 teaspoon (5 ml spoon) ground cumin
2-inch (5 cm) piece of cucumber
4–5 tablespoons (4–5 × 15 ml spoon) natural yoghurt
a little chopped parsley or chives
salt

Shell the eggs, cut in half lengthways, scoop out the yolks and arrange the whites in a serving dish. Rub the yolks through a sieve and add the cream cheese and lemon juice.

Melt the butter in a small saucepan and stir in the spices. Pour into the cheese and yolk mixture and beat until smooth. Add salt to taste and adjust the spices if desired.

Peel the cucumber, chop into small dice and stir into the cream cheese mixture. Pile the mixture into the halved egg whites and spoon a blob of yoghurt over the top of each egg. Sprinkle with chopped parsley. Chill for a short time in the fridge before serving.

Spiced Eggs with Cucumber

Chilled Almond and Chive Soup
Serves 4

This is a creamy but tangy cold soup with the delicious crunch of almonds. It is perfect for hot summer days and, since it needs no cooking, leaves you plenty of time for sunbathing.

1.1 lb (500 g) carton plain yoghurt
½ pint (300 ml) single cream
¼ pint (150 ml) milk
3 teaspoons (3 × 5 ml spoon) chopped fresh, or 2 teaspoons
    (2 × 5 ml spoon) dried, chives
2 oz (50 g) flaked almonds
salt, black pepper

Stir the yoghurt and the single cream together thoroughly until very smooth. Then stir in the milk to give the consistency of a medium-thick soup. Add the chives, followed by the flaked almonds and salt and black pepper to taste. Chill well in the fridge before serving.

Crusty Pork and Bacon Pie
Serves 8–10

There is something very rewarding about a home-made pork pie, and this pie is easy to make and particularly tasty, enhanced by the herbs and spice and the moist, sweet carrot. I find it an invaluable part of a family picnic during the summer.

For the pastry crust
12 oz (350 g) strong plain flour
½ teaspoon (2.5 ml spoon) salt
5 oz (150 g) lard
7–8 tablespoons (7–8 × 15 ml spoon) very hot water
1 beaten egg, to glaze

For the filling
1¼ lb (600 g) minced pork
½ lb (225 g) streaky bacon, with the rind removed, chopped small
1 teaspoon (5 ml spoon) coriander seeds, crushed with a rolling pin or ground in a mortar, or ½ whole nutmeg, grated
2 rounded teaspoons (4 × 5 ml spoon) finely chopped fresh sage leaves or dried oregano
½ lb (225 g) carrots, grated
salt, black pepper

First make the pastry. Put the flour and salt in a bowl and rub in the lard until the mixture has the consistency of breadcrumbs. Then stir in the hot water and knead just enough to make a very stiff dough. Leave to cool.

Grease a deep, 6–7-inch (15–18 cm) diameter cake tin, preferably one with a loose base. (Otherwise, fold an 18-inch (45 cm) strip of foil into three and lay it in the tin, leaving the two edges hanging over the sides. Grease the foil. When the pie is cooked and cooled you can remove it by lifting the two edges of the strip.) In a bowl mix the prepared filling ingredients thoroughly and season with just a little salt and plenty of black pepper.

Heat the oven to Gas Mark 3/325°F/160°C. Cut off three-quarters of the pastry. Shape into a ball and roll out on a floured surface, into a circle large enough to line the cake tin. Fit into the tin, pressing well against the sides. Spoon in the filling and press down lightly and evenly. Fold the overlapping pastry in over the filling. (If there seems too much pastry, trim a little off first.) Roll out the remaining pastry into a circle big enough to form a lid. The easiest way to make a neat circle is to place the pastry circle on top of the cake tin and press the rolling pin round the edges to cut off the excess pastry. Moisten the underside edges of the pastry lid with water and press down lightly on top of the lining pastry and filling. Roll out the trimmings to cut out decorations.

Pierce two holes in the pastry lid. Glaze with the beaten egg. Cook just below the centre of the oven for 2–2¼ hours and leave in the tin until cool. Then press out the pie and transfer carefully to a plate.

Crusty Pork and Bacon Pie

Bhikoo's Egg Dish
Serves 4

An Indian family in Delhi gave me this recipe for their favourite supper dish. The unusual combination of lightly poached eggs breaking into spiced bananas, tomato and onion gives an unexpected but delicious flavour. This is very quick to prepare: once you have chopped up the ingredients your meal can be ready within minutes.

½-inch (1.25 cm) piece of fresh ginger or ½ teaspoon (2.5 ml spoon) ground ginger
3 cloves of garlic, peeled
1 small fresh green chilli, cut open and with the seeds removed
1 large onion, sliced in thin rings
1 tomato, chopped
3 tablespoons (3 × 15 ml spoon) vegetable oil
4 bananas
½ teaspoon (2.5 ml spoon) turmeric
4 eggs
salt

Peel and chop the ginger (if using fresh ginger), garlic and chilli finely together. Heat 2 tablespoons (2 × 15 ml spoon) of the oil in a large pan and fry the sliced onion gently until soft and pale gold. Add the other chopped ingredients and sauté over a medium heat for 2–3 minutes.

Peel and slice the bananas thinly, add with the remaining tablespoon (15 ml spoon) of oil to the pan and sauté for another minute. Stir in the turmeric, and ground ginger if used.

Make four hollows in the mixture and break an egg into each. Sprinkle all over with salt, cover the pan with a lid or foil and cook over a low heat for 3–5 minutes until the whites of the eggs have just set – it is important that the yolks should not become hard. Serve straight from the pan, accompanied by a crisp green salad and toast or bread.

Buckling Pâté

Serves 4–6

If you have a liquidiser, fish pâtés are wonderfully quick to make. The cayenne, French mustard and soured cream give this one a refreshing kick. If you can't find any buckling use smoked mackerel instead.

2 whole buckling or 1 smoked mackerel
1 clove garlic, peeled
5 fl oz (150 ml) carton soured cream
2 oz (50 g) melted butter
$\frac{1}{4}$ teaspoon ($\frac{1}{2}$ × 2.5 ml spoon) cayenne pepper
1 teaspoon (5 ml spoon) French mustard
2 teaspoons (2 × 5 ml spoon) lemon juice
a little chopped parsley or fresh dill leaves
salt

Remove the skin and all possible bones from the fish and put the flesh in the liquidiser. Add all the other ingredients except the parsley and blend until smooth. (If you use dill rather than parsley, you can add a little of this to the pâté as well as sprinkling it on top.) Spoon into a pretty earthenware dish, sprinkle with the chopped parsley, cover the dish with foil and chill well in the fridge. Serve with toast or crusty bread.

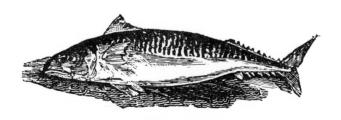

Spiced Pilaff Rice
Serves 4

This is my favourite way of cooking rice. It is glossy, golden and full of flavour, with a nutty bite to it, dotted with sweet, translucent onions. You can use it with any of the recipes in this book which suggest long-grain rice as an accompaniment, or you can make a complete dish if you have any cold chicken left over, by chopping it up and adding it to the rice for the last few minutes of cooking.

2 medium-sized onions
6 oz (175 g) long-grain easy-cook rice
1 tablespoon (15 ml spoon) cooking oil
1 oz (25 g) butter or margarine
½ teaspoon (2.5 ml spoon) turmeric
1 teaspoon (5 ml spoon) mixed spice
6 fl oz (180 ml) water
salt, black pepper

Peel the onions and chop up into small pieces. Put the rice into a sieve and wash thoroughly under hot running water.

Melt the oil and butter in a heavy-based saucepan, add the turmeric, mixed spice and the onion. Season with salt and black pepper and cook gently until the onion is just soft. Then stir in the washed rice and add the water.

Cover the pan and simmer gently for 8–12 minutes, until all the liquid has been absorbed and the rice is cooked but still has a slight bite to it. Transfer to a serving dish and serve hot.

Spiced Pilaff Rice, with Tandoori Chicken
(see p. 58)

Cheese and Onion Custard

Serves 4

I have always loved the combination of eggs and onions, and this mild soft cheese custard, which slips down your throat, topped with onions and a rich cheese sauce, is delectable. You can serve it either as a substantial first course or as a supper or lunch dish. In season a luxurious alternative is to replace the onions with cooked fresh asparagus.

For the custard
½ oz (15 g) butter
4 large (size 2 or 3) eggs
1 pint (600 ml) hot milk
2 oz (50 g) grated cheese
salt, black pepper

For the topping
1½ oz (40 g) butter
2 fairly large onions, sliced
4 teaspoons (4 × 5 ml spoon) chopped fresh, or 2 teaspoons
    (2 × 5 ml spoon) dried, chives
1 oz (25 g) plain flour
½ pint (300 ml) milk
3 oz (75 g) grated cheese
1 egg yolk
a little grated parmesan
salt, black pepper

Heat the oven to Gas Mark 2/300°F/150°C and put a roasting pan full of water in the centre. Grease a 2–2½ pint (1.1/1.4 litre) ovenproof dish with the ½ oz (15 g) butter.

Season the eggs with salt and black pepper and whisk up. Whisk in the hot milk and add the 2 oz (50 g) grated cheese. Pour into the prepared dish and place in the roasting pan of water in the oven for 1¼–1½ hours until the custard is firm.

Meanwhile, melt ½ oz (15 g) of the butter in a pan and fry the onions gently until soft. Remove from the heat and stir in the chives. When the custard is set spoon the onions and chives on the top.

Melt the remaining 1 oz (25 g) butter in a saucepan. Remove from the heat and stir in the flour. Gradually add the milk. Bring to the boil, stirring all the time, and then simmer for 2–3 minutes, stirring occasionally. Remove from the heat and stir in the 3 oz (75 g) grated cheese, adding salt and black pepper to taste. When the cheese has melted stir in the egg yolk. Pour the cheese sauce over the onions and custard, sprinkle the grated parmesan and put under a medium grill until brown.

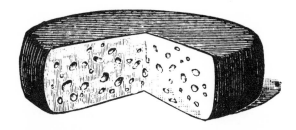

Avocados Mozzarella

Serves 4

The striped effect of pale green avocado stuffed with thin strips of white cheese under a glossy dressing makes this a beautiful and impressive first course. The melting texture of the avocado is quite delicious with the rather moist, smooth consistency of Mozzarella cheese, but if you cannot find any, another firm white cheese will do very well.

For the dressing
juice of $\frac{1}{2}$ lemon
a little over twice as much olive or sunflower oil
3 teaspoons (3 × 5 ml spoon) finely chopped fresh mint or
  2 teaspoons (2 × 5 ml spoon) dried oregano
salt, black pepper

For the avocados
2 avocado pears
1 Mozzarella cheese or 4–5 oz (100–150 g) Wensleydale or
  Caerphilly cheese

Mix together the lemon juice, oil, mint or oregano and salt and black pepper.

Cut the avocados in half, twist to separate, remove the stone and carefully peel off the skin with your fingers or a small, sharp knife. Put on plates, flat side down, and make about six or seven deep and slightly slanted cuts crossways. Slice the cheese thinly and with the help of the knife insert the slices of cheese into the cuts in the avocados.

Spoon the dressing over the top and serve.

Fresh Green Sauce

This is a cold sauce, made with fresh mint and parsley, that is excellent during the summer for pouring over and revitalising slices of cold chicken, ham, pork or veal which might otherwise be rather dull. It is also a good cold sauce for piping-hot noodles and can be used as a dressing for a cold pasta salad.

juice of 1 small lemon
¼ pint (150 ml) olive or sunflower oil
2 large cloves garlic, peeled
3 oz (75 g) fresh mint and parsley mixed
½ oz (15 g) grated parmesan
salt, plenty of black pepper

If you have a liquidiser, simply put all the ingredients in and blend until the sauce is thick and fairly smooth. Otherwise, chop the garlic, mint and parsley as finely as possible and mix thoroughly with the other ingredients.

Arrange your cold meat on a large dish and pour the sauce all over before serving.

Minty Mushrooms

Serves 4

A simple and appetising first course, always popular, and a boon to busy cooks.

¾ lb (350 g) button mushrooms, sliced thinly downwards
2 small onions, sliced very finely in rings
a large handful of fresh mint leaves, roughly chopped, or
    1 tablespoon (15 ml spoon) dried mint
3 cloves garlic, crushed or chopped finely
5 tablespoons (5 × 15 ml spoon) olive or sunflower oil
juice of 1 small lemon
1 tablespoon (15 ml spoon) white wine vinegar
salt, black pepper

Simply put all the prepared ingredients into a saucepan and season with a lot of freshly ground black pepper and a teaspoon (5 ml spoon) of salt. Mix with a spoon, cover and put the pan over a very low heat for not more than 4–5 minutes, stirring occasionally.

Pour into a serving dish, allow to cool and then store in the fridge. Serve with brown bread so that greedy people can mop up any remaining delicious juices!

Smoked Mackerel Fillets in Soured Cream

Serves 4

This effortless dish, served with fresh brown bread or slices of thin toast, makes a titillating first course to a meal. Alternatively, accompanied by a crisp salad and fresh bread, it makes a delicious light lunch during the summer.

2 smoked mackerel fillets or 1 whole smoked mackerel
juice of $\frac{1}{2}$ lemon
5 oz (150 g) carton soured cream
2–3 teaspoons (2–3 × 5 ml spoon) chopped fresh, or 2
    teaspoons (2 × 5 ml spoon) dried, chives
2–3 oz (50–75 g) button mushrooms, sliced finely
1 smallish fennel root or 2 sticks celery, sliced finely
salt, black pepper

Pull the skin off the mackerel, remove the bones if whole and cut the flesh into fairly small pieces. Put the lemon juice into a bowl and mix with the soured cream, the chives, and salt and black pepper to taste. Add the smoked mackerel, the mushrooms and the fennel root or celery.

Transfer the mixture to a serving dish. Chill in the fridge and eat the same day.

Main Courses

'If you beat spice, it will smell the sweeter.'
Sixteenth-century English proverb

Summer Chicken

Serves 6

A simple but succulent dish of golden chicken with an exciting aroma, reminiscent of a Middle Eastern feast. If your garden is overgrown with mint this is one good way to use it up!

juice of 1 lemon
2–3 tablespoons (2–3 × 15 ml spoon) olive or sunflower oil
2 large cloves garlic, crushed
1 teaspoon (5 ml spoon) ground turmeric
2–3 teaspoons (2–3 × 5 ml spoon) powdered cumin
1 large handful fresh mint leaves, chopped finely, or
　1 tablespoon (15 ml spoon) dried mint
6 joints of chicken or a 4½ lb (2 kg) chicken jointed into 6
5 oz (150 g) carton natural yoghurt
salt, black pepper

In a small bowl mix together the lemon juice, olive oil, crushed garlic, turmeric, cumin, mint and salt and black pepper. Rub or brush this mixture all over the chicken pieces. Lay them in a wide, preferably shallow, ovenproof dish. Pour over any extra oil and lemon mixture. If possible, leave to marinate for an hour or more at room temperature.

Cover the dish with foil or a lid and cook in the centre of the oven at Gas Mark 4/350°F/180°C for 1¼–1½ hours.

Before serving, spoon the yoghurt on top of the chicken. Serve with new potatoes or long-grain rice and a mixed salad.

Lamb's Liver with Paprika and Cumin

Serves 4

This is almost simple fried liver and onions but the liver is marinated to make it tender and succulent and the spices add something quite special. Of course if you can get calf's liver it is even better, and will be an extra-special treat.

1 lb (450 g) lamb's (or calf's) liver, sliced thinly
2 tablespoons (2 × 15 ml spoon) wine vinegar
5–6 tablespoons (5–6 × 15 ml spoon) olive or sunflower oil
4 tablespoons (4 × 15 ml spoon) milk
2–3 onions, sliced finely
2 cloves garlic, crushed or chopped finely
2 teaspoons (2 × 5 ml spoon) paprika
2 teaspoons (2 × 5 ml spoon) ground cumin
a handful of fresh parsley, chopped finely, for garnish
wedges of lemon for garnish
salt, black pepper

Put the slices of liver in a shallow dish or pan. Mix the vinegar with 2 tablespoons (2 × 15 ml spoon) of oil and the milk, season well with salt and black pepper and pour over the liver. Cover the dish and leave to marinate in a cool place, stirring once or twice, for several hours if possible.

Then heat 3 more tablespoons (3 × 15 ml spoon) of oil in a large frying pan and fry the onion gently until soft. Add the garlic and spices and cook for a minute or so. Adding a little more oil, if necessary, and increasing the heat, put in the marinated liver and toss for just 2–3 minutes – it is important not to overcook it.

Transfer to a serving dish, sprinkle with chopped parsley and garnish with wedges of lemon to squeeze over the liver before eating. Serve with boiled potato and parsnip (mashed together with plenty of butter, a little top of the milk, black pepper and a grating of nutmeg) and a green vegetable.

Surprise Meatballs
Serves 4

I love meatballs and there seem to be endless variations to try out. My husband suggested stuffing them with a nugget of cheese, so that as you bite into them you come across a lovely, melted centre. His favourite vegetable is spinach, and these succulent meatballs served on a bed of creamy spinach and accompanied by new potatoes make a perfect meal.

1 lb (450 g) lean minced pork or veal

2 teaspoons (2 × 5 ml spoon) dried oregano

$\frac{1}{2}$–$\frac{3}{4}$ teaspoon ($\frac{1}{2}$–$\frac{3}{4}$ × 5 ml spoon) cayenne pepper

1$\frac{1}{2}$–2 oz (40–50 g) Emmenthal or Jarlsberg cheese

2 lb (900 g) fresh, or 2 × 8 oz (2 × 225 g) frozen blocks, spinach

4–5 tablespoons (4–5 × 15 ml spoon) single cream or top of the milk

2 oz (50 g) butter

a little oil for frying

salt, black pepper

Mix the minced pork or veal in a bowl with the oregano, the cayenne pepper and a good sprinkling of salt. Cut up the cheese into small cubes. With wet hands form the meat mixture into walnut-sized balls, pressing a cube of cheese into the centre of each ball.

Now wash the fresh spinach well, put it into a large pan without extra water and cook until soft. If using frozen spinach, cook according to package instructions. Purée in a liquidiser or rub through a sieve. Add the cream, butter and salt and black pepper to taste and put into a serving dish. Cover and keep warm in the lowest oven.

Fry the prepared meatballs in a little oil over a fairly low heat for 10–12 minutes, turning them around until brown all over.

Arrange them on top of the spinach and serve. If new potatoes are not in season, bake some potatoes to go with this dish.

Spiced Duck with Prune and Hazelnut Stuffing
Serves 4–6

Duck always seems a rich, luxurious food and yet frozen duck is often surprisingly inexpensive. If it is carefully flavoured and stuffed it can be a real delicacy. You need not stick to the old stand-by of cooking the duck with oranges. For a change, spice it with cinnamon and stuff it with this moist and unusual mixture – you will then have an impressive dinner party dish without having slaved away all day preparing it.

6 oz (175 g) prunes, soaked in water overnight
2 oz (50 g) hazelnuts, chopped finely
3 oz (75 g) carrots, grated
2 oz (50 g) fresh brown breadcrumbs
2 teaspoons (2 × 5 ml spoon) ground cinnamon
1 oz (25 g) butter
4½–5½ lb duck, thawed if frozen and with the heart and liver removed and sliced finely
1–2 large cloves garlic, crushed or chopped finely
1 egg, beaten
¼ pint (150 ml) sweet dessert wine, *e.g.* Muscatel
¼ pint (150 ml) water
2 teaspoons (2 × 5 ml spoon) cornflour
salt, black pepper

Stone the prunes, chop up and put into a bowl with the prepared hazelnuts, carrot, breadcrumbs and 1 teaspoon (5 ml spoon) of the cinnamon.

Melt the butter in a small pan and toss the heart and liver with the garlic over a medium heat for 1–2 minutes. Stir into the bowl of chopped ingredients, season well with salt and black pepper and bind together with the egg. Press the stuffing right into the body cavity of the duck and skewer to enclose.

Heat the oven to Gas Mark 5/375°F/190°C. Rub the duck all over with the other teaspoon (5 ml spoon) of cinnamon and with salt. Put it on one side on a rack over a roasting pan and roast just above the centre of the oven for 40 minutes, then turn on to the other side for another 40 minutes. Finally, lay the duck on its back, breast side upwards, for another 40–50 minutes, or until it is cooked. You can test this by inserting a skewer between the leg and body – if clear juices run out it is cooked, otherwise return it to the oven.

To make a good gravy, pour the fat out of the pan and pour the dessert wine and water into the pan. Stir the cornflour in a little water until smooth and add to the wine, water and pan juices. Bring to the boil and simmer for 2–3 minutes, stirring all the time, until thickened and smooth. Season to taste.

I think plain boiled potatoes and a fresh green vegetable go best with this rich dish.

Chicken and Mushroom Paprika
Serves 4

I often make this mild, creamy dish for our supper because it is so quick and easy, but it is equally suitable for a special occasion. Serve with it either long-grain rice and a green salad or a bright green, lightly cooked vegetable such as broccoli which will look beautiful in contrast to the smooth, pinky sauce.

1 lb (450 g) boned chicken or turkey breasts
juice of 1 lemon
2 teaspoons (2 × 5 ml spoon) paprika
1½ oz (40 g) butter or margarine
6 oz (175 g) mushrooms, sliced finely or halved if small
½ pint (300 ml) single cream
a little chopped parsley
salt, black pepper

Remove the skin from the breasts and cut them into small, thin slices. Put into a bowl with the lemon juice, paprika and salt and black pepper and stir up thoroughly. Melt the butter in a large frying pan, add the chicken pieces and cook over a gentle heat, stirring now and then, for 10–15 minutes.

Add the prepared mushrooms to the pan. Then pour in the cream and stir. Heat and simmer gently for a minute or two.

Taste the sauce, add extra seasoning if needed and pour the mixture into a serving dish. Sprinkle with chopped parsley and serve.

Chicken and Mushroom Paprika

Lamb's Liver with Parsley and Buttered Leeks
Serves 4

An extremely simple dish of thinly cut parsleyed liver on a bed of buttery leeks, both nutritious and delicious. The important thing is to cut the liver as finely as possible, using your sharpest knife.

2 large leeks
3 oz (75 g) butter
1 lb (450 g) lamb's liver, sliced thinly
flour for coating
1 tablespoon (15 ml spoon) olive or sunflower oil
a handful of fresh parsley, finely chopped, or 1 tablespoon
   (15 ml spoon) dried parsley
1 small orange, cut into wedges
salt, black pepper

Remove the outer leaves from the leeks and slice very thinly in rounds. Wash well and drain. Melt 2 oz (50 g) butter in a large frying pan and fry the leeks very gently, tossing now and then, until soft. Transfer to a fairly shallow serving dish, sprinkle with salt and black pepper, cover with foil and keep warm.

Season the sliced liver with salt and pepper and dust with flour. Melt the remaining 1 oz (25 g) with the oil in the pan and toss the liver over a fairly high heat for 3–4 minutes. Then, still over the heat, add the parsley. Stir thoroughly together and then transfer to the serving dish on top of the leeks.

Decorate the border of the dish with the small wedges of orange for people to squeeze on the liver before eating. Mashed potatoes go very well with this dish.

Joints of Duck with Olives and Cinnamon

Serves 4

This is a wonderfully aromatic dinner party dish. The smell wafting from your kitchen as the guests arrive will instantly create an atmosphere of contented anticipation. It is an easy dish to prepare and can be cooked beforehand and kept warm in the oven.

4 breast and wing or leg joints of duck
2 teaspoons (2 × 5 ml spoon) ground cinnamon
1 tablespoon (15 ml spoon) olive or sunflower oil
2 cloves garlic, crushed or chopped finely
2–3 oz (50–75 g) black olives, stoned and chopped
juice of 2 oranges
$\frac{1}{4}$ pint (150 ml) water
1 oz (25 g) flaked almonds (optional)
$\frac{1}{2}$ tablespoon ($\frac{1}{2}$ × 15 ml spoon) cooking oil (optional)
a little finely chopped parsley for garnish
salt, black pepper

Heat the oven to the highest setting.

Using a large and very sharp knife cut the breast joints in half. Rub all over with the cinnamon. Heat the oil in a frying pan and fry the pieces of duck over a fairly high heat until just browned on both sides. Stir in the garlic and fry for about a minute more.

Arrange the pieces of duck in a large, fairly shallow casserole dish. Sprinkle the olives over the duck, together with salt and black pepper to taste. Pour in the orange juice and water.

Cover the dish and bring to simmering point in the oven – this should take about 15–25 minutes. Then turn down to Gas Mark 4/350°F/180°C for $\frac{3}{4}$–1 hour until the duck is tender when you insert a knife.

Pour the juices from the casserole into a saucepan and skim off as much fat as possible. Boil these juices over the highest heat until well reduced and slightly thickened –

8–10 minutes. Pour the sauce over the duck, cover and keep warm until ready to serve.

Just before serving, fry the flaked almonds, if used, in a little oil for a minute or two until golden and then sprinkle over the duck. Lastly, scatter the finely chopped parsley on top. Serve with rice and a fresh green salad or a green vegetable.

Joints of Duck with Olives and Cinnamon

Roast Pork and Spiced Apricot Stuffing
Serves 6

Stuffings are such a simple way to liven up the Sunday joint or to transform an ordinary piece of meat into a dinner party dish. The sharp yet sweet taste of dried apricots goes very well with pork and looks lovely against the whiteness of the meat.

3 oz (75 g) dried apricots
2–3 cloves garlic
$\frac{1}{2}$ teaspoon (2.5 ml spoon) ground ginger
2 teaspoons (2 × 5 ml spoon) ground cinnamon
$2\frac{1}{2}$–$3\frac{1}{2}$ lb (1.1–1.6 kg) joint of pork on the bone
a little cooking oil
$\frac{1}{2}$ pint (300 ml) dry cider
2 teaspoons (2 × 5 ml spoon) cornflour
salt, black pepper

Chop the apricots and garlic together very finely. Put them into a bowl and throughly mix with the ginger and cinnamon. Press this mixture into any gaps in the meat and into deep pockets made with a sharp knife. Rub the joint all over with oil and the crackling with coarse salt.

Put into a hot oven, Gas Mark 8/450°F/230°C, for 20–30 minutes, or until the crackling is beginning to brown and crisp. Then turn down the oven to Gas Mark 3/325°F/160°C and roast for another 2–$2\frac{1}{2}$ hours, basting occasionally.

Half an hour before the meat is ready, pour the excess fat from the pan and add the cider and salt and black pepper to taste. When the meat is cooked, remove it from the pan, blend the cornflour with a little water until smooth, stir it into the pan juices and boil on top of the cooker for about 2 minutes. This will make a delicious gravy.

Serve with roast or new potatoes and vegetables.

Marrakech Meatballs

Serves 4

One of my favourite Moroccan dishes is these simple meatballs, which are served with eggs lightly cooked in the same dish at the last moment. The taste when the egg yolk breaks into the spiced meat and juices is quite delicious.

$\frac{3}{4}$ lb (350 g) minced lamb or beef
I oz (25 g) ground rice or semolina
I teaspoon (5 ml spoon) cinnamon
I–2 cloves garlic, crushed or chopped finely
I beaten egg
2 oz (50 g) butter or margarine
I tablespoon (15 ml spoon) tomato purée
I teaspoon (5 ml spoon) paprika
$\frac{1}{4}$ pint (150 ml) water
4 eggs
salt, black pepper

Pound the meat with a wooden spoon or blunt-ended rolling pin in a bowl to make it as soft and smooth as you can. Add the ground rice or semolina, cinnamon, garlic, I teaspoon (5 ml spoon) of salt and black pepper. Bind the mixture together with the beaten egg. With wet hands form the mixture into small balls about the size of a marble.

Melt the butter or margarine in a pan and fry the meatballs until just browned all over. Transfer them to a fairly wide, shallow ovenproof dish or a small roasting pan and pour the fat over them. Mix the tomato purée and paprika with the water, season with salt and black pepper and pour over the meatballs.

Heat the oven to Gas Mark 4/350°F/180°C. Cover the dish with foil or a lid and cook in the centre of the oven for 40–45 minutes. Then break the eggs into the dish, spaced out among the meatballs. Cover the dish again and put back in the oven for 8–10 minutes, only until the whites of the eggs have just set. (If you make this dish in advance, keep it warm at a low heat, then add the eggs and turn up the heat again to cook them just before you are going to eat, to ensure that the yolks are still nice and runny.) Serve with long-grain rice and a salad.

Marrakech Meatballs

Tandoori Chicken

Serves 6

This famous Indian way of roasting chicken pieces is traditionally carried out in a huge clay oven in which the heat is generated by charcoal at the base. However, a successful imitation can be achieved in an English kitchen and is always popular, even with the children.

6 chicken joints
juice of 2 lemons
4–6 cloves garlic
1 small piece (about 1 inch, 2.5 cm) fresh root ginger, peeled and chopped, or 2 teaspoons (2 × 5 ml spoon) ground ginger
1 teaspoon (5 ml spoon) pickling spice
$\frac{1}{2}$ teaspoon (2.5 ml spoon) cumin seeds or ground cumin
$\frac{1}{2}$ tablespoon ($\frac{1}{2}$ × 15 ml spoon) white wine vinegar
5 oz (150 g) carton natural yoghurt
2 teaspoons (2 × 5 ml spoon) paprika
1 oz (25 g) butter
salt

Wash and dry the chicken joints. Make deep cuts in the joints and rub all over with salt and some of the lemon juice. Allow to marinate for half an hour at room temperature.

Either blend in a liquidiser the garlic, ginger, pickling spice, cumin seeds, the rest of the lemon juice, vinegar, yoghurt and paprika, or grind the garlic, ginger, pickling spice and cumin seeds in a pestle and mortar (or between two sheets of greaseproof paper, using a rolling pin) and then mix with the lemon juice, vinegar and yoghurt, lastly adding the paprika. Smear this paste all over the joints, cover and again leave to marinate, this time for at least 8 hours or overnight, putting in the fridge if the weather is at all warm.

When the marinated chicken is ready heat the oven to Gas Mark 6/400°F/200°C. Remove any excess marinade from the chicken joints, place in a roasting pan, dot with the butter and roast for 20 minutes in the centre of the oven. Then sprinkle joints with the remaining lemon juice, baste with the melted butter and grill both sides, for about 5 minutes each side, under a hot grill. Garnish with finely sliced onion rings, wedges of lemon and chopped fresh mint leaves, and serve with pilaff rice (see p. 32) and a mixed salad.

Trout with Herb and Cream Stuffing

Serves 4

In this delicate dish the trout are poached in white wine and filled with a soft herb, butter and cream stuffing which imparts its gentle flavour to the rest of the fish. The juices are delicious with new potatoes and baby carrots.

4 oz (100 g) butter
2 oz (50 g) plain flour
3 teaspoons (3 × 5 ml spoon) white wine vinegar
3 tablespoons (3 × 15 ml spoon) single cream
2–3 teaspoons (2–3 × 5 ml spoon) fresh, or 2 teaspoons
    (2 × 5 ml spoon) dried, thyme
4 rainbow trout, thawed if frozen
2 small onions, very finely sliced in rings
¼ pint (150 ml) white wine
salt, black pepper

Beat 3 oz (75 g) of the butter until soft. Then beat in the flour, followed by the vinegar and cream, season well with salt and black pepper and stir in the thyme. Spoon the mixture into the gutted body cavity of each trout.

Heat the oven to Gas Mark 6/400°F/200°C. Using ½ oz (15 g) more of the butter, grease a rectangular ovenproof dish and lay the trout in it. Scatter the sliced onions on top and dot with the remaining butter. Pour over the wine and cover the dish with foil. Bake in the centre of the oven for 40–45 minutes, or until cooked through.

Trout with Herb and Cream Stuffing

Chicken Roasted in Yoghurt

Serves 4–6

This way of roasting a chicken produces a very succulent flavour. You can vary the taste by adding your own choice of herbs, garlic or spices to the yoghurt – it is particularly good with curry paste stirred into it. Here is one version which everyone seems to like.

$3\frac{1}{2}$–$4\frac{1}{2}$ lb (1.6–2 kg) chicken, well thawed if frozen
juice of 1 lemon
2 teaspoons (2 × 5 ml spoon) ground cinnamon
2 teaspoons (2 × 5 ml spoon) fresh, or 1 teaspoon (5 ml spoon) dried, thyme
5 oz (150 g) carton natural yoghurt
salt, black pepper

Make deep cuts in the breast and legs of the chicken and sprinkle with the lemon juice. Leave for at least half an hour at room temperature to allow the juice to penetrate the flesh.

Heat the oven to Gas Mark 6/400°F/200°C. Then mix the cinnamon, thyme and salt and black pepper into the yoghurt and spread thickly all over the chicken. Roast in the centre of the oven for $1\frac{1}{4}$–$1\frac{1}{2}$ hours, until cooked. Cover the breast with foil if it browns too quickly.

Serve with new potatoes or buttered noodles and fresh courgette or broccoli.

Pork Tenderloin Rolled with Cheese and Sage

Serves 2

I love this dish. It almost melts in your mouth and although it is so easy to make, mouths will water as you cut through and reveal the layers of oozing cheese and delicate lean meat. Small new potatoes and a spinach purée are perfect with it.

¾ lb (350 g) pork tenderloin
¼ whole nutmeg, grated, or ¼ teaspoon (½ × 2.5 ml spoon)
   ground nutmeg
a good handful of fresh sage leaves, chopped finely
4 oz (100 g) Emmenthal, Gruyère or Danish Fynbo cheese
1 oz (25 g) butter
5 oz (150 ml) carton soured cream
grated parmesan
salt, black pepper

Heat the oven to Gas Mark 3/325°F/160°C. Put the tenderloin between two sheets of wet greaseproof paper and beat with a rolling pin until approximately ¼ inch (5 mm) thick. Remove the paper, lay the meat out and sprinkle all over with the nutmeg and salt and black pepper, followed by the sage. Then slice the cheese as thinly as possible and lay the slices evenly on top of the sage. Roll up the meat from the shortest end, folding over the edges to enclose the cheese, and secure with a wooden toothpick if necessary.

Put the roll into a fairly shallow ovenproof dish, dot with butter, cover with foil or a lid and cook for 1–1¼ hours, until the juices run clear when a skewer is inserted in the centre, and the cheese has just begun to ooze out. Just before serving, spoon the soured cream over the top of the roll and sprinkle generously with grated parmesan.

Pork Tenderloin Rolled with Cheese and Sage

Breast of Chicken Coriander

Serves 4

This aromatic dish is quick to prepare but put it together several hours before you cook it so that the chicken has time to absorb the delicious, mild spices. The resulting creamy mixture of tender chicken breast and celery topped with crunchy cashew nuts goes well with new potatoes or rice and a simple green salad.

1 lb (450 g) boned chicken (or turkey) breasts
2 teaspoons (2 × 5 ml spoon) coriander seed
1-inch (2.5 cm) piece fresh green ginger or ½ teaspoon (2.5 ml spoon) ground ginger
2 cloves garlic
2 tablespoons (2 × 15 ml spoon) tomato purée
juice of 1 lemon
3 tablespoons (3 × 15 ml spoon) sunflower or other cooking oil
1 small head celery, sliced finely in rings
5 fl oz (150 ml) carton single cream
4 oz (100 g) cashew nuts
salt, black pepper

Remove the skin from the chicken breasts and cut them across in fairly thin slices. Grind the coriander seed in a pestle and mortar, or between two sheets of greaseproof paper with a rolling pin. Cut the skin off the fresh ginger and peel the cloves of garlic, and finely chop both together. Put into a mixing bowl with the ground coriander, tomato purée, lemon juice and 2 tablespoons (2 × 15 ml spoon) of the oil. Season with salt and black pepper and stir. Then stir in the sliced chicken and celery. Cover the bowl with a cloth and leave to marinate in the fridge overnight, or about 8 hours.

Pre-heat the oven to Gas Mark 4/350°F/180°C. Transfer the mixture to a fairly shallow casserole dish and stand at room temperature for about half an hour. Then cover and cook in the centre of the oven for 50–

60 minutes. Stir in the cream and put back in the oven for a further 5–10 minutes – just enough to reheat. Finally, fry the cashew nuts in a little oil until just golden and scatter over the chicken before serving.

Green Chilli Veal

Serves 4

This is a tender, smooth casserole with a mild bite of chilli and the lovely flavour of sweet peppers. Serve it with long-grain rice or new potatoes, accompanied simply by a green salad.

2 small fresh green chillies
1–2 cloves garlic, peeled
1½ oz (40 g) butter or margarine
2 tablespoons (2 × 15 ml spoon) cooking oil
1 lb (450 g) pie veal, cut into cubes
2 fairly large red peppers or pimentoes, sliced thinly in rings
2 rounded tablespoons (4 × 15 ml spoon) plain flour
½ pint (300 ml) chicken stock
5 fl oz (150 ml) carton soured cream
1 teaspoon (5 ml spoon) paprika
salt

Cut the chillies open and remove all the seeds. Then chop the chillies and garlic together very finely. Melt 1 oz (25 g) of the butter or margarine with the oil in an iron casserole dish or large frying pan and stir in the chilli, garlic, veal and red peppers. Stir until coated in butter and oil and season with salt. Add the flour and stir in the stock.

Heat the oven to Gas Mark 1/275°F/140°C. Bring to the boil, stirring all the time, and then cover the casserole (or transfer the mixture from the frying pan to a hot ovenproof casserole dish) and cook in the oven for 1¼ hours, or until the meat is tender. Then stir in the soured cream.

Melt the remaining ½ oz (15 g) of butter in a small pan and add the paprika to it. Trickle this red liquid over the top of the casserole just before serving.

Green Chilli Veal

Spiced Lamb with Apricots
Serves 4

This is a delectable lamb stew, reminiscent of a Moroccan *Tagine* – a stew cooked in the traditional pointed earthenware pot. It has a rich, mildly spiced sauce and is perfect with pilaff rice (see recipe on p. 32).

4 chump end lamb chops
1 tablespoon (15 ml spoon) cooking oil
2 cloves garlic, crushed or chopped finely
1 heaped teaspoon (5 ml spoon) ground cinnamon
1 teaspoon (5 ml spoon) ground ginger
1 large onion, chopped
2 oz (50 g) dried apricots
1 teaspoon (5 ml spoon) paprika
1 oz (25 g) flaked or split almonds
salt, black pepper

Trim the excess fat off the meat.

Heat the oil in a heavy-based saucepan. Add the garlic, cinnamon, ginger and onion and stir. Then add the meat and apricots and enough water (approx. 1 pint, 600 ml) to more or less cover the meat. Cover the pan, bring to the boil and simmer very gently for about 1½ hours, or until the meat is tender and beginning to fall away from the bone. Then strain the juices off into another saucepan and arrange the meat, apricots and onions in a serving dish and keep warm.

Stir the paprika into the juices, bring to the boil and bubble fiercely for 5–10 minutes until the sauce is reduced and thickened. Season to taste with salt and black pepper and spoon over the meat. Fry the almonds until golden in a little oil in a frying pan, sprinkle on top of the meat and serve.

The Memsahib's Curried Chicken
Serves 4

In India a housewife will never use ready-made curry powder: each day she will grind her own combination of spices for the daily meal. In this way the curries of India are more personal and the freshly ground spices give a tantalising aroma and a far superior flavour. This recipe is my own version of dishes I saw prepared while on a journey in India – tender chicken joints wrapped in a mildly spicy, creamy, rich sauce. If you like your curries really hot you just increase the quantity of fresh ginger and chilli.

1-inch (2.5 cm) piece of fresh ginger or 1 teaspoon (5 ml spoon) ground ginger
1 small green chilli
1 large clove garlic
2 cardamom pods or 1 teaspoon (5 ml spoon) coriander seeds
juice of $\frac{1}{2}$ lemon
1 tablespoon (15 ml spoon) natural yoghurt
4 chicken joints, thawed if frozen
2 tablespoons (2 × 15 ml spoon) cooking oil
2 hard-boiled eggs, shelled and sliced
salt

For the sauce
1 tablespoon (15 ml spoon) dried milk powder
5 tablespoons (5 × 15 ml spoon) single cream
5 tablespoons (5 × 15 ml spoon) natural yoghurt
chopped parsley, to garnish

Roughly peel the fresh ginger, if used, and cut open the chilli and discard all the seeds. Then peel the garlic and chop all these ingredients together as finely as possible. Remove the seeds from the cardamom pods if used and grind these or the coriander seeds in a pestle and mortar, or crush with a rolling pin between two sheets of grease-proof paper. Mix the lemon juice and the tablespoon (15 ml spoon) of yoghurt together and stir in the prepared

71

spices, including the ground ginger, if used. Score the chicken joints all over with a knife and coat all over with the yoghurt and spice mixture. Leave in a covered dish to marinate overnight, or for several hours, in the fridge. Then sprinkle the joints with salt to season.

Heat the oven to Gas Mark 4/350°F/180°C. Heat the oil in a pan and fry the joints over a medium heat until pale golden on both sides. Transfer to a casserole dish with the oil and spices from the pan. Cover the casserole and cook in the oven for ¾–1 hour, or until cooked. Then transfer the chicken joints to a warm serving dish and arrange the slices of hard-boiled egg amongst them.

Pour off any excess fat from the casserole juices and boil the juices in a saucepan for 2–3 minutes until reduced and thickened. Stir in the milk powder, cream and the 5 tablespoons (5 × 15 ml spoon) of yoghurt and heat gently but don't boil. Pour the sauce over the chicken and sprinkle with chopped parsley. Serve with long-grain rice or new potatoes, and a salad.

The Memsahib's Curried Chicken

Sharp Steak and Mushroom Stew

Serves 4

This effortless dish shows that with the right seasoning and long slow cooking even a simple beef stew can become rich and full of flavour.

1¾ lb (800 g) stewing steak
2 tablespoons (2 × 15 ml spoon) plain flour
2 teaspoons (2 × 5 ml spoon) soft brown sugar
¼ whole nutmeg, grated, or ½ teaspoon (2.5 ml spoon) ground nutmeg
2 teaspoons (2 × 5 ml spoon) fresh rosemary leaves or 1 teaspoon (5 ml spoon) dried rosemary
1 large onion, sliced
½ pint (300 ml) water
1 tablespoon (15 ml spoon) Worcestershire sauce
2 tablespoons (2 × 15 ml spoon) tomato ketchup
1 tablespoon (15 ml spoon) wine vinegar
¼ lb (100 g) mushrooms, sliced
a little parsley, chopped
salt, black pepper

Heat oven to Gas Mark 2/300°F/150°C. Cut the meat into cubes and put into a casserole dish. Stir in the flour thoroughly. Then add all the other ingredients except the mushrooms and parsley. Stir together and season with salt and black pepper. Cover the dish and cook in the oven for 2½–3½ hours, until tender, stirring occasionally. Add the mushrooms 15 minutes before the end.

Just before serving, sprinkle the chopped parsley over the top of the stew. Serve with baked potatoes and buttered carrots.

Turkey in Puff Pastry

Serves 4–6

Meat wrapped in a glazed pastry case is always an impressive dish to serve at a dinner party, although using packet puff pastry it is simple to prepare. In this recipe the breast of turkey stuck with thyme and a little garlic is covered with a layer of liver sausage or pâté, then encased in the crisp golden pastry and served with a soured cream sauce. Remember to start it in good time, as the meat has to be precooked and cooled before the pastry stage.

1 clove garlic
4 teaspoons (4 × 5 ml spoon) fresh, or 2 teaspoons (2 × 5 ml spoon) dried, thyme
2 lb (900 g) breast fillet of turkey, rolled and tied up
cooking oil
$\frac{1}{4}$ pint (150 ml) vermouth or white wine
8 oz (225 g) continental liver sausage or soft liver pâté
13 oz (367 g) packet frozen puff pastry, thawed
1 egg yolk
1 teaspoon (5 ml spoon) cornflour
5 fl oz (150 ml) carton soured cream
salt, black pepper

Heat the oven to Gas Mark 3/325°F/160°C. Chop the garlic finely and mix with the thyme. Press the mixture deep into the gaps in the meat with your fingers. Cover the meat generously with oil and sprinkle all over with salt and black pepper. Roast the joint in the centre of the oven for about 2 hours, basting occasionally and adding the wine to the pan about half an hour before the end.

Take out the meat and leave to cool completely, reserving the juices in a small saucepan. When the meat is cold cut off the string.

Heat the oven to Gas Mark 6/400°F/200°C. Take the skin off the liver sausage and press it (or the pâté, if used) all over the meat, making the surface as even as possible. Roll out the pastry to a piece big enough to wrap the meat in, about 15 inches (38 cm) square. Lay the meat in the centre, cut off a 2-inch (5 cm) square at each corner, dampen the edges and wrap up the joint like a parcel, making sure that there are no more than two thicknesses of pastry in any one place. Cut decorations from the pastry trimmings.

Put the pastry parcel in a greased roasting pan and brush all over with the egg yolk. Cook in the centre of the oven for 25–35 minutes, until a rich golden brown and puffed up.

Before serving, blend the cornflour with a little cold water and stir with the soured cream into the pan juices. Bring gently to the boil, stirring until thickened. Test for seasoning and add salt, pepper and a little more thyme if you wish. Pour into a sauce boat and serve with the meat. I normally serve new potatoes with this dish and broccoli, broad beans or a good mixed salad.

Turkey in Puff Pastry

Spare Rib Pork Chops and Fresh Herb Sauce
Serves 4

The creamy sauce, made with a tasty concentration of fresh herbs, transforms this simple dish of fried pork chops. Accompanied by new potatoes, the sauce is also perfect for fried or grilled lamb or fish.

4 spare rib pork chops
2 tablespoons (2 × 15 ml spoon) cooking oil
1–2 large cloves garlic, crushed
¼ pint (150 ml) milk
2 teaspoons (2 × 5 ml spoon) cornflour
a handful of fresh mint leaves, chopped
a small handful of fresh tarragon or 2 sprigs rosemary,
     stripped from the stalks and chopped
¼ pint (150 ml) single cream
juice of 1 lemon
salt, black pepper

Sprinkle the chops with salt and pepper. Heat the oil in a large frying pan, brown the chops and, reducing the heat, fry them slowly over a low heat with the garlic, for 10–15 minutes on each side, or until cooked and tender. Then transfer them to a serving dish and keep warm in a low oven.

Put the milk in a saucepan with any juices from the frying pan. Blend the cornflour in a little water until smooth and add to the milk. Bring to the boil, stirring, and simmer for 2–3 minutes. Add the herbs, and simmer for a moment more. Finally, stir in the cream and lemon juice with salt and black pepper to taste. Pour over the chops on the serving dish and serve immediately.

Creamy Chicken Pasta

Serves 4–6

A delicious way of serving pretty shaped pasta – shells, spirals and sometimes even bows. If you cannot find the shaped pasta, of course, you can use flat noodles. It is a perfect dish for a family meal as children love it quite as much as the adults do.

10 oz (300 g) pasta shapes
1½ oz (40 g) butter
1 tablespoon (15 ml spoon) cooking oil
10–12 oz (300–350 g) boned chicken breast, skinned and cut into 1-inch (2.5 cm) pieces
1 medium-sized onion, chopped
¼ lb (100 g) mushrooms, sliced finely
½ pint (300 ml) single cream
2–3 teaspoons (2–3 × 5 ml spoon) fresh, or 2 teaspoons (2 × 5 ml spoon) dried, chopped tarragon
salt, black pepper

Boil the pasta in plenty of salted water according to package instructions or for 10–15 minutes, until tender. Drain and rinse through with hot water. Put into a serving bowl and stir in ½ oz (15 g) of the butter. Cover and keep warm in a very low oven while you make the sauce.

Melt the remaining 1 oz (25 g) butter with the oil in a large frying pan and toss the chicken pieces in it over a fairly high heat for 3–4 minutes. Add the chopped onion and cook over a lower heat until the onion is just soft. Then add the sliced mushrooms, tossing for another minute. Finally add the cream, tarragon and plenty of salt and pepper. Allow the cream to get just hot and then mix the sauce with the pasta. Serve with a salad.

Pork Chops with Green Pepper and Garlic Sauce
Serves 4

This is a recipe for a sauce which is equally good with fried or grilled fish, lamb, veal or chicken. Please don't be put off by the quantity of garlic. You will find that used in this way it will not flavour too strongly; its main purpose is to amalgamate the sauce, which includes no flour.

4–5 cloves garlic, unpeeled
4 lean pork chops
$\frac{1}{2}$ oz (15 g) butter or margarine
3 tablespoons (3 × 15 ml spoon) olive or sunflower oil
2 fairly large green peppers, cored and chopped into small pieces
juice of 1 small lemon
salt, black pepper

Boil the garlic cloves in a pan of water for 15–20 minutes, until soft. Meanwhile, season the chops with salt and pepper. Melt the butter and 1 tablespoon (15 ml spoon) of the oil in a large frying pan, brown the chops and then fry over a rather low heat for 7–10 minutes on each side, until the pork is cooked through. Transfer the meat to a serving dish and keep warm in a low oven.

Add the chopped peppers to the pan juices and cook, still over a low heat, until softened, stirring fairly often. Add the lemon juice and the remaining 2 tablespoons (2 × 15 ml spoon) of oil to the pan and allow just to heat. Sprinkle with salt and black pepper.

Now squeeze the softened garlic cloves out of their skins into a liquidiser and spoon in the peppers, lemon and oil mixture. Blend until smooth and thick or rub through a sieve with a wooden spoon. Either pour over the chops or serve separately in a small dish.

If necessary, cover the dish(es) with foil and keep warm in a low oven until ready to serve. Serve accompanied by new potatoes and either broad beans or a tomato salad.

Desserts and Gâteaux

'And lucent syrops, tinct with cinnamon;
Manna and dates, in argosy transferr'd
From Fez; and spiced dainties, every one,
From silken Samarkand to cedar'd Lebanon'
John Keats, 1795–1821

Gooseberry and Mint Pie

Serves 4–6

This is an example of what the taste of fresh mint can do for sweet dishes, as well as savoury. If you dislike gooseberries you can make this pie with any other sharp-flavoured stewing fruit, according to season. Blackcurrants are very good. The rich and crumbly pastry always works well, so even if you don't consider yourself a pastry cook, do try it.

For the pastry
8 oz (225 g) plain flour
2 tablespoons (2 × 15 ml spoon) icing sugar
4 oz (100 g) butter or margarine
2 oz (50 g) lard
1–2 tablespoons (1–2 × 15 ml spoon) very cold water

For the filling
1½ lb (700 g) fresh or frozen gooseberries
1 tablespoon (15 ml spoon) chopped fresh, or ½ tablespoon (½ × 15 ml spoon) dried, mint
3 oz (75 g) sugar
a little caster sugar

Make the pastry in advance. Sift the flour and icing sugar into a bowl. Cut the fat into the flour and rub in with your fingertips until it is like breadcrumbs. Stir in the cold water until the mixture just begins to stick together. Knead into a ball, wrap in foil and chill in the fridge for at least an hour.

Preheat the oven to Gas Mark 6/400°F/200°C. Top, tail and wash the gooseberries. Put them in a round, shallow 8-inch (20 cm) pie dish, with a pie funnel in the centre if you have one. Mix the chopped mint with the sugar and sprinkle it evenly over the gooseberries.

Roll out the pastry on a lightly floured surface to about ¼ inch (5 mm) thick. Dampen the edge of the pie dish and carefully put the pastry on top. Trim the edges neatly and use the trimmings to decorate. Cut a slit or cross in the centre of the pastry for the steam to escape. Brush the surface with water and sprinkle with a little caster sugar.

Bake in the centre of the oven for 30–35 minutes. The pastry should be golden – if it is getting too brown place a piece of foil on top. Serve hot or cold, with cream.

Orange Butter Spice Biscuits

Makes approx. 6 dozen biscuits

This American method of biscuit-making is so convenient. The roll of rich, soft dough will keep firm in the fridge for up to a fortnight. Just cut thin slices from it as you like, whenever you want a batch of freshly made biscuits. Within 10 minutes you will be nibbling these crisp, light biscuits, which are a perfect accompaniment to ice cream and fruit fools. The quantities given here will make at least three batches of biscuits.

4 oz (100 g) butter
7 oz (200 g) caster sugar
1 large (size 2 or 3) egg
finely grated rind of 1 orange
8 oz (225 g) strong plain flour
2 teaspoons (2 × 5 ml spoon) mixed spice
½ teaspoon (2.5 ml spoon) salt
2 teaspoons (2 × 5 ml spoon) baking powder

Beat the sugar and butter until light and creamy. Thoroughly beat in the egg. Add the orange rind. Sift the flour with the spice, salt and baking powder and stir into the butter and egg mixture. Flour your hands and shape the dough into one long or two short rolls, about 2 inches (5 cm) thick. (If you find the dough too soft to shape, put it in the fridge until it is more manageable.) Wrap the roll in foil or cling-film and chill for at least 3 hours, more if possible.

To cook, heat the oven to Gas Mark 5/375°F/190°C, take the roll of dough from the fridge and, using a sharp knife, slice off about 10–12 thin rounds and arrange on the baking sheet – well spaced out. Bake in the centre of the oven for 7–9 minutes, until a pale golden colour. Remove biscuits while hot with a palette knife and place on a cooling rack whilst still warm. Repeat with the rest of the dough when required, until it is all used up.

Apple Lattice Tart

Serves 4–6

Cinnamon has long been used to great effect in the cooking of apples. This pretty apple tart, with its rich, sweet pastry and tangy purée of apples, has a crisp cinnamon glaze on the top. It is a lovely treat for all the family.

For the pastry
6 oz (175 g) strong plain flour
2 tablespoons (2 × 15 ml spoon) icing sugar
good pinch of salt
3 oz (75 g) butter or margarine
2 oz (50 g) lard

For the filling
1 lb (450 g) cooking apples
2 tablespoons (2 × 15 ml spoon) golden syrup
juice of 1 lemon
1 oz (25 g) butter
1 egg, separated
1 teaspoon (5 ml spoon) ground cinnamon
2 teaspoons (2 × 5 ml spoon) caster sugar

First make the pastry. Sift the flour, icing sugar and salt into a bowl. Cut in the fat and crumble with your finger-tips until the mixture resembles rough breadcrumbs. Now add just under a tablespoon (15 ml spoon) of very cold water and stir the mixture with a knife until it starts to stick together. Press into a ball, wrap in cling-film or foil and chill in the fridge for at least an hour.

Peel and core the apples and cut into chunks. Put them in a saucepan with the golden syrup and lemon juice. Cover and simmer very gently for 10–15 minutes until soft and mushy. Stir in the butter until melted. Cool the mixture slightly, blend in a liquidiser until smooth, or rub through a sieve, and then allow to cool completely.

Cut off about two-thirds of the pastry, knead slightly, shape into a ball and roll out on a floured board into a circle to line an 8–9-inch (20–22 cm) shallow flan dish, preferably the metal kind with a loose base. Roll the rolling pin over the top edge of the dish to cut off the excess pastry neatly. Prick the base lightly with a fork. Mix the egg yolk (reserving the white) into the apple purée and spoon the mixture into the flan case. Roll out the remaining pastry and cut into ten ½-inch (1 cm) strips, re-rolling if necessary. Arrange half the strips over the top, spaced equally, and the other five diagonally over them, and leave the edges hanging over the dish. When finished, press the rolling pin round the edges to cut off the overlapping pieces.

Heat the oven to Gas Mark 5/375°F/190°C. Add the caster sugar and the cinnamon to the reserved egg white and whisk lightly with a fork. Brush thickly over the lattice top and bake the tart in the centre of the oven for 35–40 minutes, until a rich golden brown. Serve warm or cold, with cream.

Lemon Spice and Strawberry Delight

Serves 6

This is a delicious dessert. Underneath a topping of fresh strawberries (or you can use raspberries) there is a light, mousse-like lemon layer over a tangy custard. Try to make it in a glass ovenproof dish so that you can see the three layers. When soft fruit is out of season you can simply serve it on its own or sprinkle grated chocolate on top, whilst on cold days it is wonderful served hot with a chocolate sauce or cream.

2 oz (50 g) butter
8 oz (225 g) caster sugar
juice and grated rind of 2 small lemons
4 eggs, separated
2 oz (50 g) self-raising flour
$\frac{1}{4}$ whole nutmeg, grated, or $\frac{1}{4}$ teaspoon ($\frac{1}{2}$ × 2.5 ml spoon) ground nutmeg
8 fl oz (250 ml) milk
$\frac{1}{2}$ teaspoon (2.5 ml spoon) cream of tartar
$\frac{3}{4}$ lb (375 g) small fresh strawberries
icing sugar

Butter a $2\frac{1}{2}$–3 pint (1.4–1.7 litre) ovenproof dish. Put a roasting pan half full of water in the centre of the oven and heat at Gas Mark 4/350°F/180°C.

Cream the butter until soft, add the caster sugar and beat until fluffy. Beat in the lemon juice and rind and then the egg yolks. Sift the flour and nutmeg together and stir in. Gradually stir in the milk and beat or whisk the mixture thoroughly until very smooth.

Add the cream of tartar to the egg whites and whisk until standing in soft peaks. Fold gently into the lemon mixture with a metal spoon.

Pour into the dish, put this into the pan of water in the oven and bake for 35–40 minutes, until golden brown on top. Leave to cool and then arrange the strawberries on top. Serve with cream if you like.

Strawberries in Ginger and Orange Cream

Serves 4–6

This is a mouthwatering way to serve strawberries and especially good if you haven't got quite enough to go round. The orange juice seems to enhance the flavour of the fruit and the slightly sharp-tasting cream, combined with the crystallised ginger, makes it a luscious dish. When the strawberry season is over you can use raspberries, loganberries, and later blackberries in the same way.

1 lb (450 g) strawberries
½ pint (300 ml) double or whipping cream
2–3 tablespoons (2–3 × 5 ml spoon) caster sugar
5 oz (150 g) carton natural yoghurt
juice of 1 small orange
2 oz (50 g) crystallised or stem ginger, chopped finely

Take the stalks off the strawberries and halve them if they are large. In a large bowl whip the cream until thick and then stir in the sugar to taste, the yoghurt and, gradually, the orange juice. Carefully stir the strawberries into the mixture together with the ginger. Transfer to a bowl, preferably a pretty glass one. Chill in the fridge before serving.

Raspberry and Walnut Spice Gâteau

An irresistible dessert! This very light and yet nutty cake, shining with a sharp jelly glaze, is sandwiched together with whipped cream and fresh raspberries – a beautiful treat.

3 oz (75 g) plain flour
1½ teaspoons (3 × 2.5 ml spoon) baking powder
1 teaspoon (5 ml spoon) mixed spice
¼ teaspoon (½ × 2.5 ml spoon) salt
3 large (size 1 or 2) eggs
3 oz (75 g) soft brown sugar
2 oz (50 g) finely chopped walnuts and a few half-walnuts
  for decoration
¼ pint (150 ml) double or whipping cream
8 oz (225 g) fresh or thawed frozen raspberries
1 tablespoon (15 ml spoon) orange or redcurrant jelly
2 teaspoons (2 × 5 ml spoon) lemon juice or water

Lightly oil two 7–8-inch (18–20 cm) sandwich tins and lightly dust with flour. Line each with a disc of oiled greaseproof paper. Heat the oven to Gas Mark 4/350°F/160°C.

Sift the flour with the baking powder, spice and salt two or three times and put on one side. Put the eggs into a deep bowl standing over a large pan of very hot water. Whisk until thickish and a pale lemon colour. Then whisk in the brown sugar and continue whisking until the mixture has greatly increased in volume and is thick enough to stand in peaks. (Of course, this is all much quicker if you can use an electric whisk.) Then, using a metal spoon, very lightly fold in the chopped walnuts. Sift the flour once again on top and gently cut and fold into the mixture.

Pour the mixture into the prepared tins and bake in the centre of the oven for 15–20 minutes until risen and well browned. Let the cakes cool in the tins. When cool, loosen the sides with a knife and turn out, removing the greaseproof paper.

Whisk the cream until thick. Put the cake on a serving plate and sandwich together with the whisked cream and all but a few of the raspberries. Gently melt the jelly with the lemon juice or water and stir until smooth (if you have any home-made crab apple or quince jelly the flavour will be particularly good). Brush the top of the cake with the liquid jelly and decorate with the remaining raspberries and the half-walnuts.

Keep in a cool place but preferably not the fridge, unless you are saving the gâteau for next day. If so, take it out of the fridge for at least half an hour before serving.

Spicy Gâteaux: Chocolate Cinnamon Gâteau (see p. 94) and Raspberry and Walnut Spice Gâteau

Chocolate Cinnamon Gâteau

This is my idea of a perfect chocolate cake: moist, rich and gooey, covered with whipped cream and trickles of melted chocolate. It is much more of a pudding than a cake and always seems to disappear quickly.

5 oz (150 g) plain chocolate
6 tablespoons (6 × 15 ml spoon) water
4 oz (100 g) butter or margarine
5 oz (150 g) soft brown sugar
3 large (size 1 or 2) eggs, separated
2 oz (50 g) ground almonds
2 oz (50 g) fresh white breadcrumbs
1 teaspoon (5 ml spoon) ground cinnamon
apricot jam
¼ pint (150 ml) double or whipping cream

Grease a fairly shallow 7–8-inch (18–20 cm) cake tin and line with a disc of greased greaseproof paper. Melt 4 oz (100 g) of the chocolate in the water and stir until smooth. Leave to cool slightly.

Beat the butter until soft. Add the brown sugar and beat until fluffy. Beat in the egg yolks, followed by the ground almonds and the melted chocolate. Stir in the breadcrumbs and cinnamon.

Heat the oven to Gas Mark 5/375°F/190°C. Whisk the egg whites until they stand in soft peaks. Then, using a metal spoon, fold them gently into the chocolate mixture and spoon evenly into the prepared cake tin. Bake in the centre of the oven for 40–50 minutes, until springy to a touch in the centre. Cool completely in the tin.

When cool, loosen the edges with a knife and turn out. Melt the remaining chocolate with 1 tablespoon (15 ml spoon) more water. Stir until smooth and leave to cool. Put the cake on a serving plate and spread all over with apricot jam. Whisk the cream until thick and with it ice first the sides and then the top of the cake in rough flicks. Then, holding the spoon high above the cake, trickle the cooled chocolate over it in thin criss-cross patterns. Leave in a very cool place, preferably not the fridge, until ready to serve.

The Author

Josceline Dimbleby was born in Oxford in 1943. From the age of five her childhood was spent abroad, mostly in the Middle East and South America, so that at an early age she learned to appreciate a wide variety of food.

Josceline's instinct has always been to create her own recipes, which results in varied and interesting dishes, but leading a very busy life herself she appreciates the value of advance preparation and simple methods and most of her recipes reflect this view without in any way affecting their originality.

Josceline regularly writes cookery articles for the national press and has featured on television and radio. Her first cookery book, *A Taste of Dreams*, appeared in 1976, followed in 1977 by *Party Pieces*, a booklet for the Victoria and Albert Museum's Silver Jubilee Exhibition of Young British Craftsmen. *Cooking with Herbs and Spices* is the third in her series of cookbooks for Sainsbury's, following *Cooking for Christmas* and *Family Meat and Fish Cookery*.

Josceline lives in London with her husband, journalist and broadcaster David Dimbleby, and their three children.